JAZZ-ROCK FUSION

VOLUME

II

Jazz Rock Fusion Vol 2
LES DeMERLE

Publisher
NDA PUBLICATIONS

"great drum books from great drummers"

PO Box 626
N Bellmore, NY 11710
phone 516-735-2984
fax 516-735-2995
email ndadrum@aol.com

Exclusive Worldwide Distribution

HAL LEONARD CORPORATION

7777 W Bluemound Road   Box 13819
Milwaukee, WI 53213

Acknowledgements
Julie Oldfield-Musical Typist
Tom Copi-Photos
Ann Giuliano-Typeset
Vito Lupo-Cover Design
Doug Garrison-Sambandrea Swing Transcription
Tad Weed-Pianist & Friend-Assistance on blues charts for piano, bass & drums
Special Thanks-Al Miller, Jerry Ricci, Dom Famularo
This Book is Dedicated to Maiya for her constant inspiration

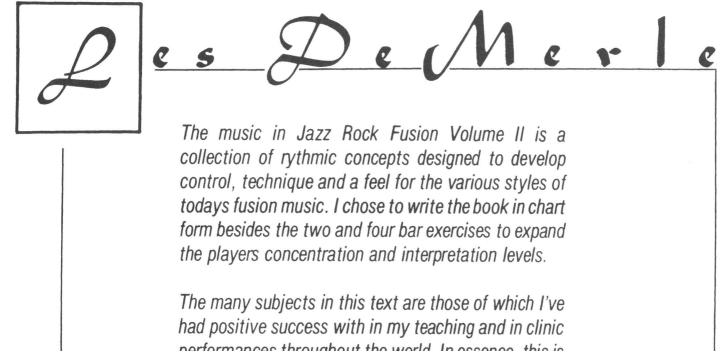

Les DeMerle

The music in Jazz Rock Fusion Volume II is a collection of rythmic concepts designed to develop control, technique and a feel for the various styles of todays fusion music. I chose to write the book in chart form besides the two and four bar exercises to expand the players concentration and interpretation levels.

The many subjects in this text are those of which I've had positive success with in my teaching and in clinic performances throughout the world. In essence, this is a thesis of jazz rock work, for the player to develop an independent, contemporary concept.

Les De Merle

LES DeMERLE

JAZZ-ROCK FUSION

VOLUME II

PARADIDDLE JAZZ INVERSIONS FOR SET

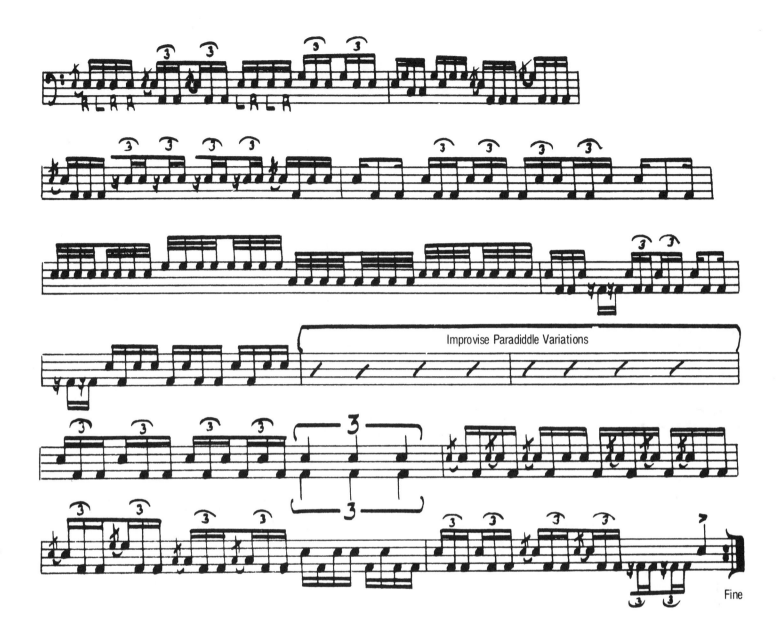

Improvise Paradiddle Variations

Fine

HI-HAT, BASS DRUM INDEPENDENCE

♩ = 100

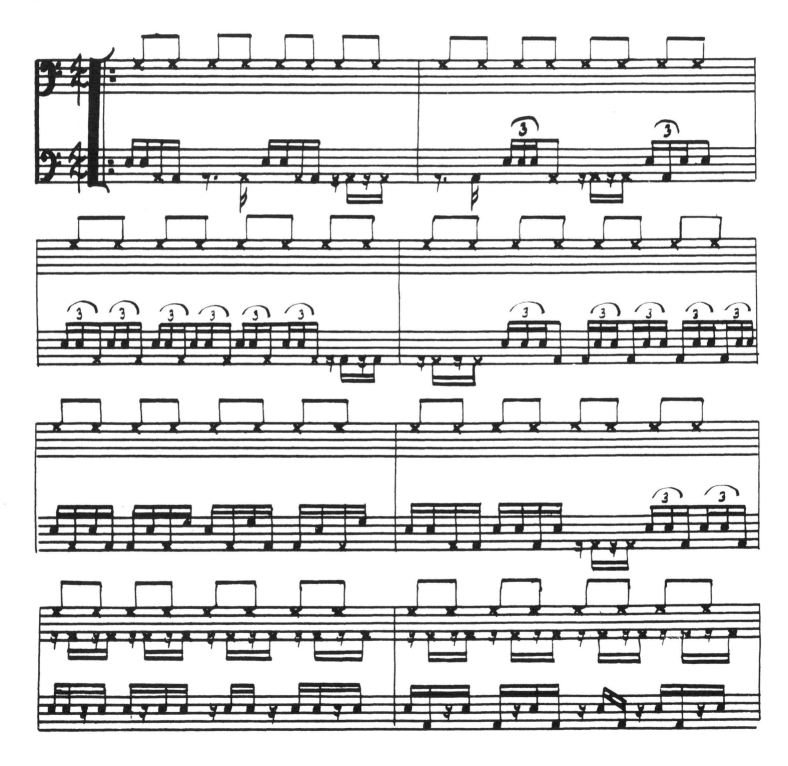

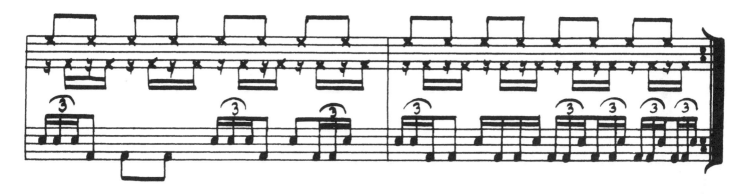

Doug Norwine   Kevin Brandon   Don Menza
Ramsey Embick   Les   Ralph Rickert

FUNK IN 7/4 INDEPENDENCE EXERCISE

♩ = 92

SAMBA JAZZ GROOVE

♩ = 144

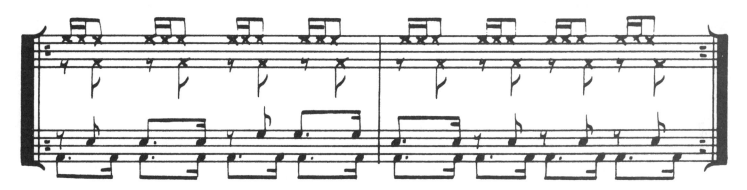

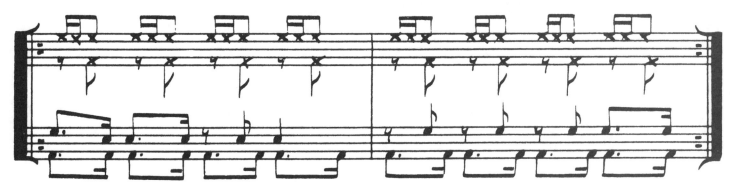

VARIATIONS ON BOSSA NOVA FEELS
4/4 and 3/4

♩ = 132

VARIATIONS ON BOSSA NOVA FEELS

5/4

♩ = 132

JAZZ VARIATIONS
4/4 and 3/4

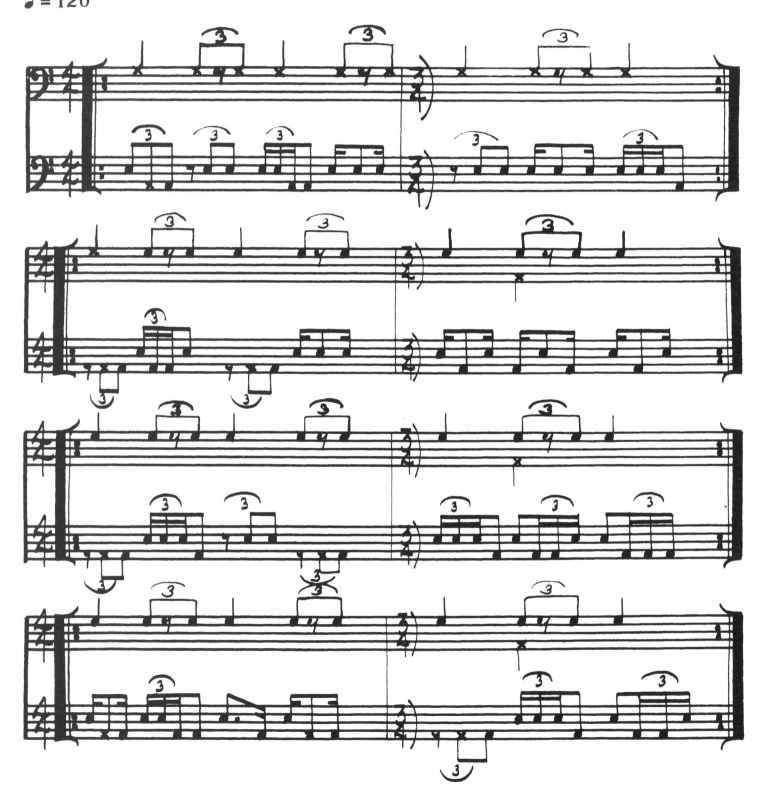

SIGHT-READING INTERPRETATION WITH A JAZZ FEEL

♩ = 116

JAZZ WALTZ

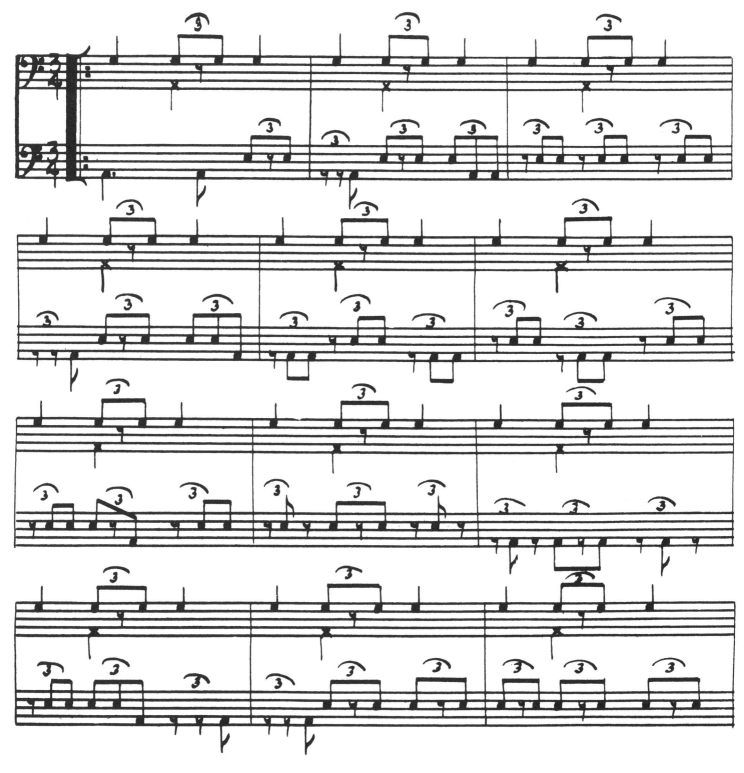

29

JAZZ SNARE DRUM SOLO

♩ = 112

VARIATIONS

7/8

(OVER THE BAR PHRASING)

TWO-BAR SNARE AND BASS JAZZ INDEPENDENCE LINES

5/4

♩ = 138

TWO-BAR SNARE AND BASS JAZZ INDEPENDENCE LINES

♩ = 138

4/4

THREE-BEAT PHRASING
UNDER THE JAZZ RIDE RHYTHM
4/4

♩ = 120

FIVE-BEAT PHRASING
UNDER THE JAZZ RIDE RHYTHM
4/4

♩ = 120

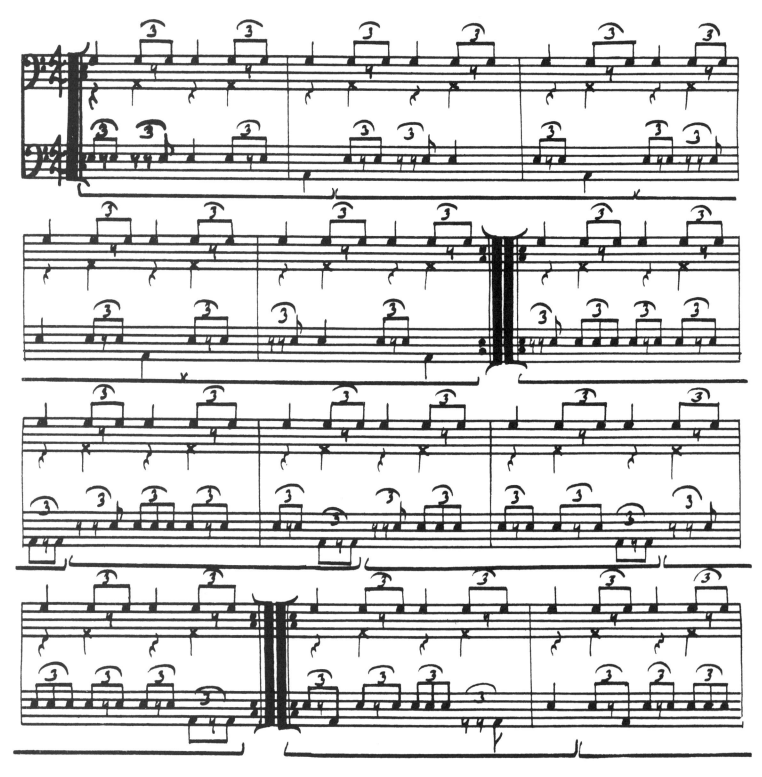

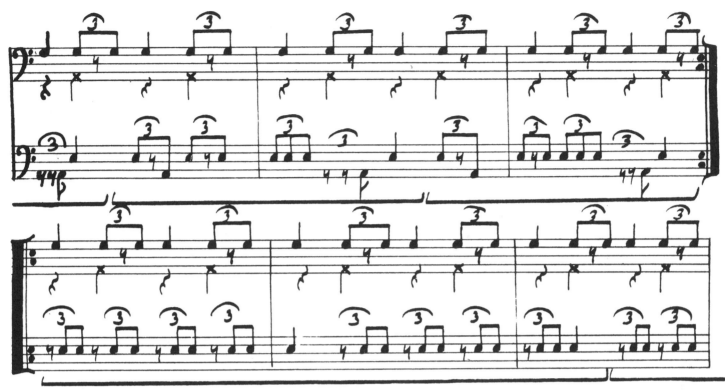

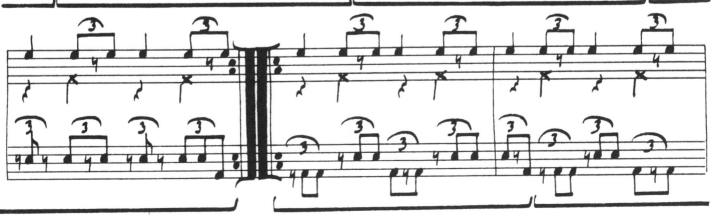

Small Tom   Snare   Bass Drum   Big Tom

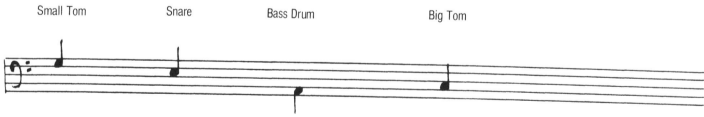

TWO-BAR SYNCOPATED FUNK VAMPS

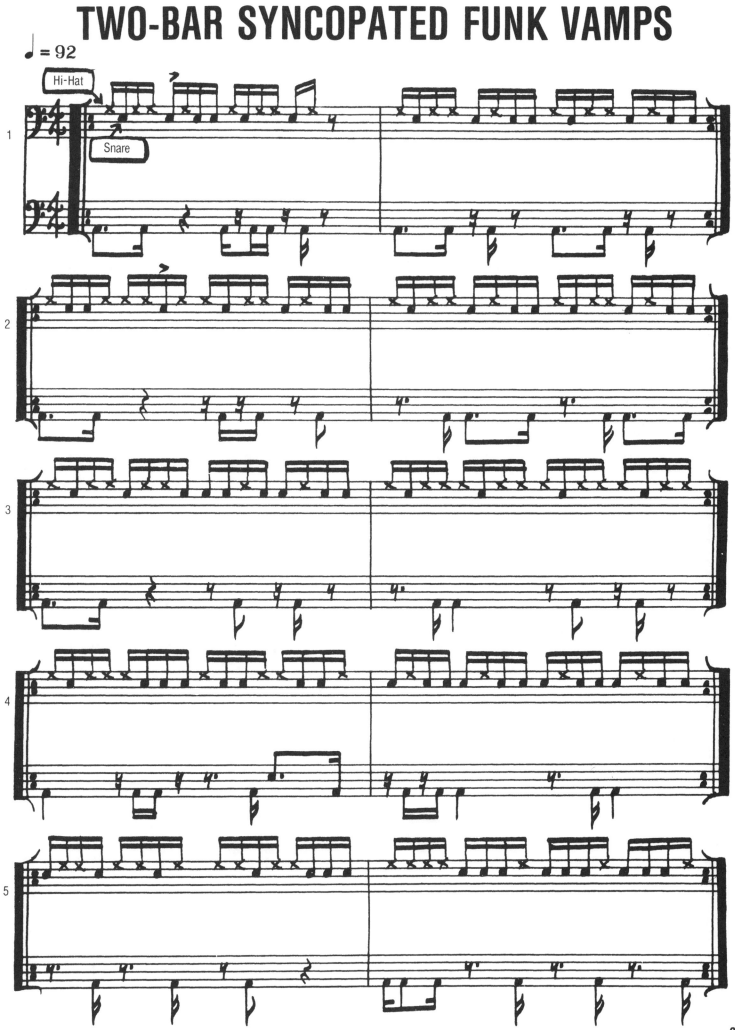

OPEN HI-HAT WORK IN A TIGHT 16TH-NOTE FUNK FEEL

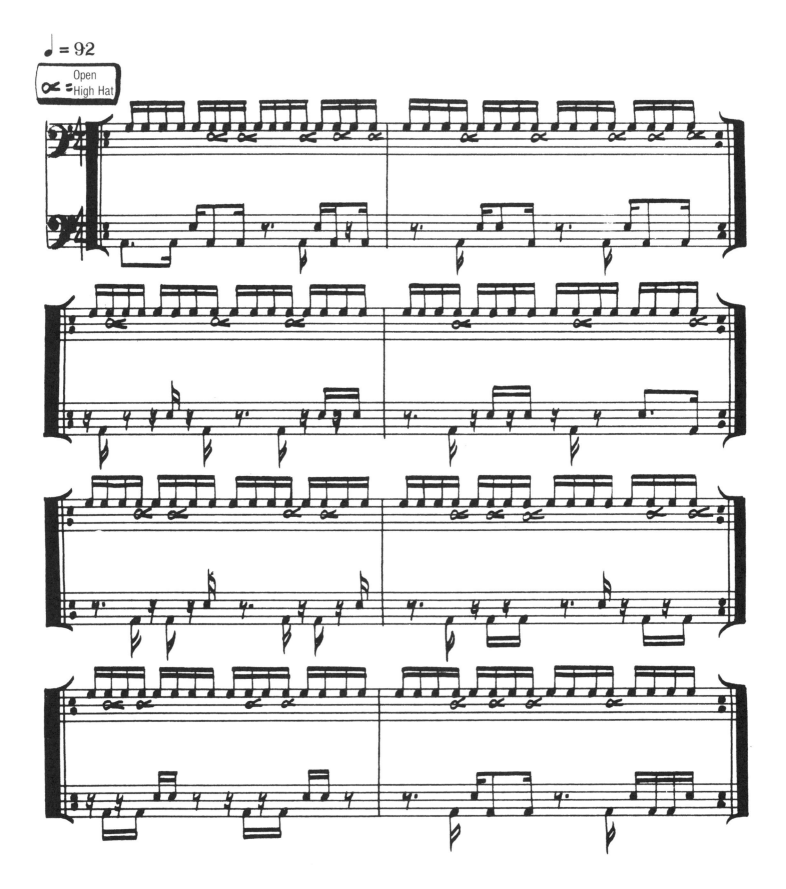

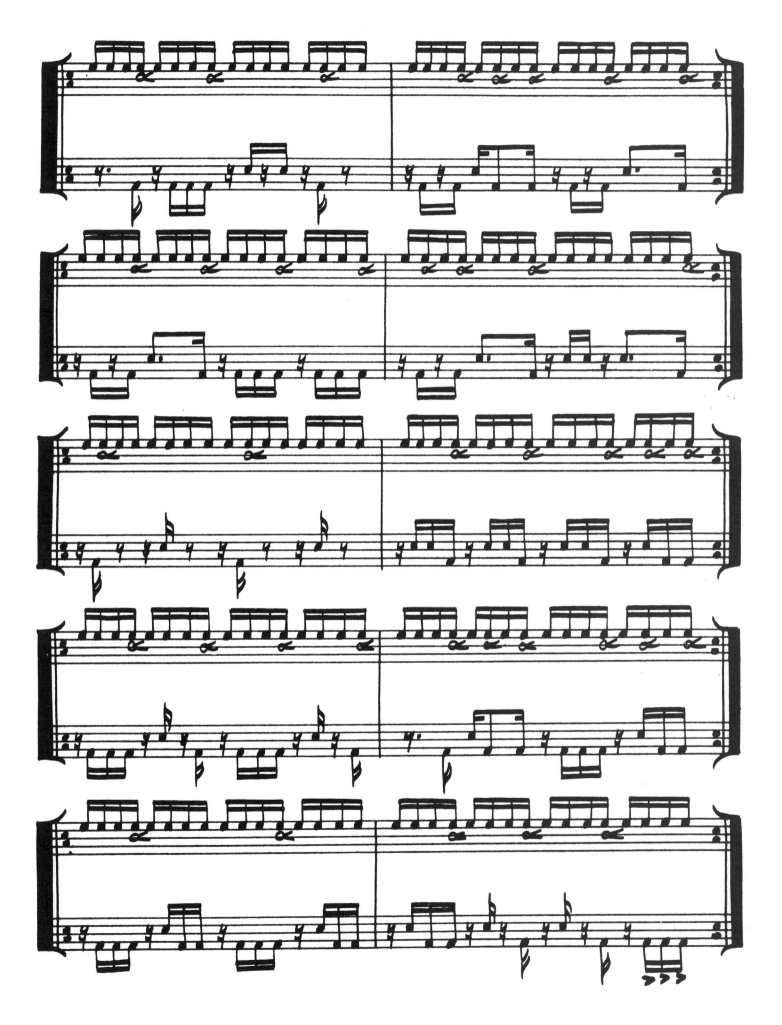

LES DE MERLE'S IMPROVISED SOLO ON
SAMBANDREA SWING

From:
*LIVE AT CONCERTS
BY THE SEA L.P.*

Transcribed by
DOUG GARRISON

B.D. Pattern Cont'd.

BLUES FUSION ONE

Composed by Les DeMerle

♩ = 132

PIANO

BASS

BLUES FUSION ONE
BLUES FOR FIVE DRUMS

♩ = 132

Composed by Les DeMerle

TUNING FOR DRUMS

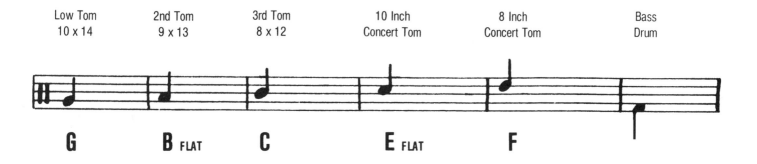

Low Tom 10 x 14	2nd Tom 9 x 13	3rd Tom 8 x 12	10 Inch Concert Tom	8 Inch Concert Tom	Bass Drum
G	**B** FLAT	**C**	**E** FLAT	**F**	

BLUES AT MIDNIGHT

♩ = 100
PIANO

Composed by Les DeMerle

BASS

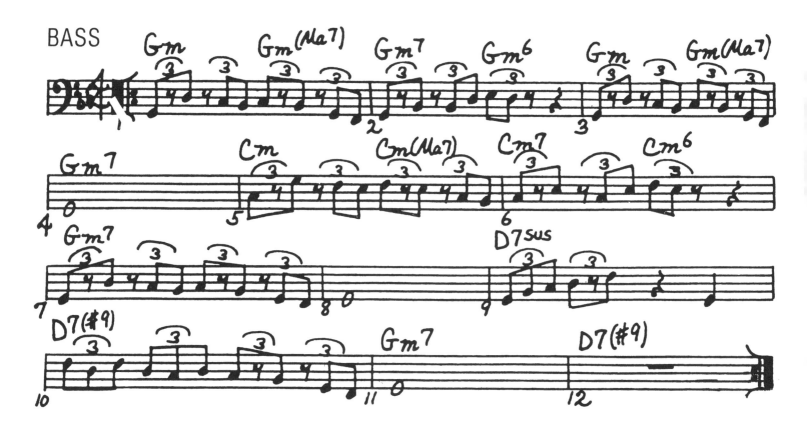

BLUES AT MIDNIGHT
BLUES FOR 7 DRUMS

Composed by Les DeMerle

TUNING FROM HIGH TO LOW DRUMS
CONCERT TOMS

8 Inch Tom	10 Inch Tom	12 Inch Tom	13 Inch Tom	14 Inch Tom	15 Inch Tom	16 Inch Tom
G	F	D	C	B FLAT	G	F

BLUES FOR ELVIN

Dedicated to Elvin Jones

Composed by Les DeMerle

BLUES FOR ELVIN
BLUES FOR 8 DRUMS

Dedicated to Elvin Jones

Composed by Les DeMerle

♩ = 192

FAST BLUES

TUNING FROM HIGH TO LOW DRUMS
CONCERT TOMS

6 Inch Tom	8 Inch Tom	10 Inch Tom	12 Inch Tom	13 Inch Tom	14 Inch Tom	15 Inch Tom	16 Inch Tom

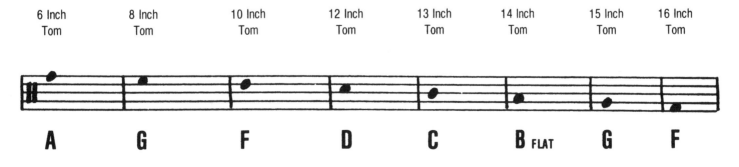

| A | G | F | D | C | B FLAT | G | F |

AFRO FUSION BLUES

Composed by Les DeMerle

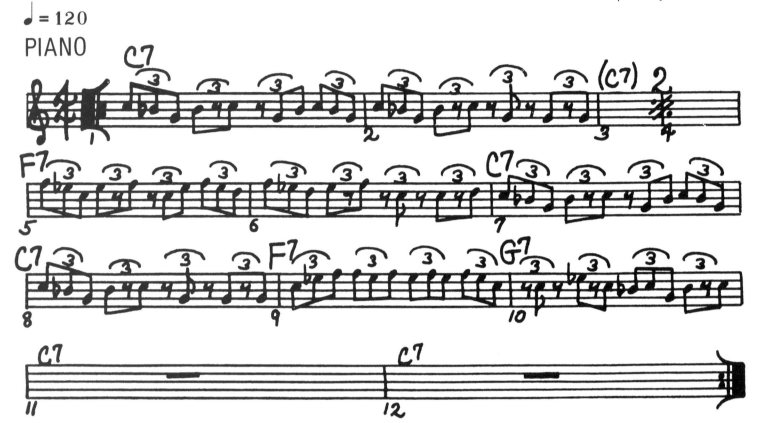

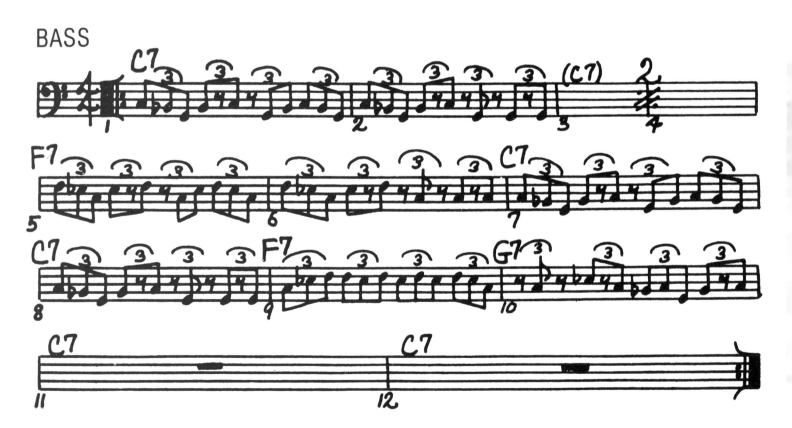

AFRO FUSION BLUES
BLUES FOR 5 DRUMS

Composed by Les DeMerle

Les, Congratulations on a very musical follow up to Jazz-Rock Fusion Volume I. Jazz-Rock Fusion Volume II covers more styles and sets more trends in contemporary drumming.

— Al Miller

Thankfully we accept this new contribution from the tiger of Transfusion. It should certainly inspire and stimulate or; on the other hand, perhaps discourage a whole generation of young drummers. Congratulations Les — you've got a whole lot going for you.

— Jim Chapin